The Wild Field

The
Wild Field

poems by
Rita Gabis

ALICE JAMES BOOKS
CAMBRIDGE, MASSACHUSETTS

Acknowledgments

Acknowledgment is made to the following journals and anthologies in which some of these poems first appeared:

Beloit Poetry Journal: "Missouri." *Cape Discovery: The Provincetown Fine Arts Work Center Anthology,* Sheep Meadow Press: "The Woodpile." *Chester H. Jones:* "Father." *Columbia Magazine:* "Washing Beans." *Ironwood:* "Blood," "The Voice." *Passages North:* "Leaving," "Wishes." *Provincetown Arts:* "Laundry and Wind." *Puerto del Sol:* "I Make A Place Here." *Yellow Silk:* "Sleeping Together," "Solitude," "These Eggs," "Letter."

I am grateful to The Fine Arts Work Center in Provincetown, Massachusetts; the Corporation of Yaddo; and the Millay Colony for the Arts for residencies which aided in the completion of this work.

Epigraph:
Reprinted from "Domestic Interior" by Eavan Boland, in *Outside History: Selected Poems 1980-1990,* with the permission of W.W. Norton & Company, Inc. Copyright © 1990 by Eavan Boland.

Library of Congress Catalog Card Number 93-49828
ISBN 1-882295-01-3

Alice James Books gratefully acknowledges support from the National Endowment for the Arts and from the Massachusetts Cultural Council, a state agency whose funds are recommended by the Governor and appropriated by the State Legislature.

Alice James Books are published by the Alice James Poetry Cooperative, Inc.
Alice James Books
33 Richdale Avenue
Cambridge, Massachusetts 02140

for Harriet Quaker-Franklin
and for Mike

Contents

One

Two

Three

Four

Love is also memory.
—*Eavan Boland, "Domestic Interior"*

The Wild Field

One

I Bring In The Last

Summer cuttings,
strip them

of leaves. They litter the table
with gold dust, these

deceivers, thin-stemmed, silly
petal heads blooming

into November. Their faces touch
ground, their long stalks are whipped

by north wind
and bow

as in obedience.
Even broken, they flower

beyond all reason.
Lavender, vermillion

in the weed crib,
the dirt

harbors of wild seed.
My mother's flowers

grow by the barn.
Their tall spines shimmer.

Color, trace of blood
on my thigh. When I no longer

keep time
by the dull, loved ache

of it, may I
teach a daughter

to gather from the node,
to weather blossoms

beyond their first season.
And in the cold

when I shudder,
my failures unadorned

by heat,
may I honor my own beauty

among wind-falls, the clutch
and scroll of empty pods,

dry treasures with a purpose
beyond memory.

And fill my arms with late-blooming cosmos
until their weight

becomes palpable, set in the crook
of my steadfast vanities, dreams.

Leaving

I remember the slender points of the petals,
but not the windowsill where the bowl was placed,
if it was spring or full summer, if it was
my hand that cupped the blossom out of the water,
its odor of wind and bark, the stamen's sweetness.
The girl who sunburned her breasts by the bay
and brought men back to the house
at night, when the dogstar flowered, who was she?
And made love to them in a room above her mother's room,
above the broken stem from the tulip tree,
the pale, pink scent left there when
she kissed them goodbye, a light scarf over the lamp
softening faces with shadow.
Did her father ever pass the thin-branched
shadows of the budded limbs, did he come
home finally across cricket-studded grass
and stare through the torn screen of the kitchen window?
And if I was there, in the bed upstairs,
semen ribboned on my thighs as first light rubbed out
stars, and dew chilled the five-petaled life
on the sill and outside, did I kiss my own wetness
left on the sex of the man, did I hold the flower to my face
at the end of the night, barefoot on the stripped
boards of the kitchen floor, where no one woke
or returned to the threshold, whispered
my name in the throat of the blossom,
told me to go?

Fireflies

I'm reading about fireflies, remembering
the joy these tiny beetles have given me in fields
when I thought I was alone, and first one came on
and then another.

By the shadows of wild carrot, in weeds,
on the bark of maples, they shine with cold light
after months, years without wings. Only nothing, hunger
in the sticky body, a tiny white groove in the earth,
sleeping and waking in darkness.

They wait until the end of their lives to glow
a sexual fire, a signal
so the female will know where the male is among
redolent grasses and runaway clover.
They come to their senses and die.
And then more lights flicker by the stone heaps
of ancient fences, over the ridges my shoes make at dusk.

How plain they were in the jam jar, brought in, examined
beneath the porcelain light in the kitchen. Grandmother
was not an old woman then, she turned the gold
lid with five straight fingers, all this excitement
over brown wings and a simple body. I'm thinking

about fireflies. The more I know of them,
the happier I am without wings or fire,
with the heat my body creates when I stand with my back
to the stars, wrists in shadow, knees chilled
by a cool wind. And lonely, I speak to
the flickering, white, umber, green
with a dark and human voice.

Gold Bowl

After the first rising, I punch down
the bloated bread dough.
The gluten toughens and sighs
in the old gold bowl my mother gave me.
It holds the shapeless weight,
the yeast, the sticky stuff that clings
to my long spoon and fingers.
She never told me women become what they make.
I'm cold milk poured in a glass. I'm sweet
black molasses. I'm wheat flour scattered
about the waist and feet.
Once a week she calls
to tell me she is hungry.

As a child I loved the story
of vagabond soup, made from water
and a nail. Whoever comes to the table
adds to the pot that simmers on the back
of the stove all day. Home,
my spoon clacked against the side of the dish.
My mother's food wounded me.

I prepare a feast for my loved ones, cut
hot bread. The steam gathers and falls.
It's raining in a small place in the kitchen.
I salt the blood in the stew, pepper my lips
and arms. I make too much at every meal,
leftovers to spoon into the mouths of ghosts,
their crevices and grief holes.
Ghost of my mother's mother,
the smallest wind shook the stick of her spine.
Of her twenty Siberian winters
hauling brick, I know only the food she ate;

black bread, potatoes, gift of milk
from a guard. I scrape off the fat,
their losses dirty-white
like old river ice.

There is a hole in the bottom of the bowl.
I have to remind myself not to climb
down the doughy convex sides, to keep
kneading the muscle out of the wheat,
minding the places where the skin breaks
because the spirit of the bread can disappear
like the spirit of a woman.
Mother calls to me from the gold well,
her thin voice almost lost
in the shadows.
I won't go down there,
I won't become just another hunger
dressed in women's clothes.

Father

I thought he knew about darkness.
Within it the corn was shifting, the stalks full
on the wind, the air I was breathing warm,
the gravel road shone white by the fences.
I thought he was with me there though he was
sleeping. I didn't understand his arms
were the arms of a man, with their sun-marks
and shadows. I thought he knew
about the stars I saw above the blue water tower
each evening, why they kept moving away from me.
I thought he could hear what I said
to the pump that looked like a bird at night,
to the clothes-line turning in the shape of a tree,
as I tried out my voice after the moon
reached the top of the barn, saying *hello, hello*
to the things I believed I was tied to, the scratch-grass,
the sunflowers. I thought he could carry
the moon. But a man can't carry the moon,
a man cries into his fists,
made out of bone, made out of water.
I'd put on my father's shirts when they were old,
mixing my odor with his, rubbed into
the cloth from his walking, his reaching, his stooping,
his breathing, and it did not make me stronger.

Washing Beans

I love the feel of beans in water,
beautiful in the colander, bright as stones
after low tide is over and the salt wash rises
and covers the sides they bare to the moon.
The skins split from the red ones and wrinkle,
the round black ones might have fallen from a star.
I could pray to the white ones, they are so ordinary.
I think of each bean as a life, we were born
in the same field, between two poles,
two extremities of cold. I live for simple things,
the lump under one arm that is nothing;
oil from sweat the doctor said, life isn't meant
to be easy. I stand at the sink, my hands covered with
three kinds of beans. This is the anniversary
of my friend's death. I remember his last haircut.
He didn't feel the universe resting on his shoulder,
the seed start to split, the skin pull back from the bones
until the soul wandered out. I don't have the heart to say
beans have no meaning. They will not be lost to me.
They might be the eyes of wind, they might be kidneys.
They have no ghosts, but they have shadows, and come back
as roots or the gourd's armor or stone.

Lesson In A Language I Can't Speak Yet

The jellyfish lies naked on the sand,
a circle I can see through to the bright harvest
of stones. On one side of it is white foam,
on the other black seagrass.
A gold line of sunlight circles the bay.
I don't know how the life of a jellyfish begins,
I don't know where its sex is,
or why the circle is its shape among
all the shapes in the world. The flesh-colored
armor of crabs dries on wet sand.
The snail retreats when I touch it.
The footprints I leave here are full of the vanished
weight of the body.
The heart of the jellyfish is clear,
I was born deaf to the sounds it makes, its cells that shine
next to the rough arms of the starfish,
the starfish that can regenerate
its severed limbs. I have entered
another country, where lost parts of myself re-form;
hatred from the same salty center as love,
desire that had been torn from me.
I have to be open to powers
I know nothing about.
Identity in small things,
the jellyfish that smells like the sea,
the sea that touches all corners of the earth at once,
holes in the sand where mussels breathe.

Grandmother In The Garden

Her bones whittled sharp as thorns,
she works all day, stabs
runaway roots of day lilies, beds peonies in seaweed,
black confetti I've helped her gather at low tide.
Don't be like me, I've had a horrible life,
her pink skull just starting to show under
thick white hair, hands crabbed, fortune
good or bad whorled in each palm.
Hands that dug the sour ground of a family,
planted chokecherries and ash trees,
freesia so sweet it hurt
to breathe it in. She built a searock wall
to keep disorder out, the flood
as each of her children came, acorns
she plucked up, hating the little tree sprouts,
as I have bent over my own body and seen only scars,
wept because the rain wouldn't stop or start
when I begged it to. I've drunk her potions,
steeped all night in coppery water,
to keep life fluid in a rigid spine,
straight as the sticks she trained roses with.
Once I tugged on the thread of her workdress,
sun-bleached, smelling of dry earth and salt.
The loose stitching will break free,
and I won't know where it started, only that at the end
of loneliness lies loneliness; the source
of the blossoming will root deeper into memory.

The Voice

The voice of a man I don't know comes back to me.
Maybe I heard it on the radio, or turning
into the dark on the street that runs away
from the crosswalk, maybe I heard it there,
words spoken from the shadow of a hat brim
as I was going somewhere, a voice under
a black umbrella if it was raining.
I'm not even certain of what
he was saying, or why it was a man and not
a woman, because I love the voices of women.
I don't even know if it was today
that I heard it for the first time,
but it was a question, it was a man asking
in sounds pressed out of all he had seen
and been given, something as
insignificant as *pass the salt,* at a table
I did not know I would think about later,
or the same man asking something
plain on a street, needing to know the north
and south of the lights and the evening,
as I needed a voice I loved
without knowing whose it was
or what he was saying.

Gift

I took everything from my mother, her liquor, her ghosts,
her sweetness, her heavy lips, her breath of sorrow.
I took her waist and her spools, her ears and her thimble,
I took her green thumb, and the purple cosmos blossoms
that trembled under her kitchen window.
I took her feet and her loneliness, the cities
she lived in, the small towns, their friendless dusks,
her quilts and perfumes and fingers.
I took the sound of her dresses at midnight,
and the goat she kept as a child,
I took the crickets beneath the boards of her first houses
and her lovers; I got lost in their shadows.
I took her hatred of her father,
I ate from her dishes in rooms that smelled of the sea.
I took the war and the horses that pulled the cart
that carried her mother away.
I took the odor of crushed thyme and sweat,
I took a handkerchief embroidered by my great-aunt
and the iron in her shoulder and the road signs
of old villages.
I took my mother's maiden name and her fear of oceans,
I took her bravery and her strangeness,
I took a blessing from her and
the lullabies she whispered, drunk,
and my terror of that dark music.
I took my love for a woman
who walked through a broken doorway
with her eyes closed,
following no one.

Missouri

Lying out in the switch grass
to feel the ground-echo
of a train eating away
the flatland dark of Missouri;
Cairo, Paris, Mexico,
county-talk dry
as a locust shell.

At night on a brick street,
I sat on the tar patch
of the roof, rubbing
moonlight into my hair—
the night pollen,
hoping to be changed.

Scent of a mud-bottomed river
still on my skin,
born in the wrong town,
born from the wrong family,
given the wrong name.

After midnight,
oak smell in the cool air,
the dry winds shifting,
chaff, the clang
of a silo side, drum-shadow
of a water tank in starlight.

Cabin Fever

Third day of snow, a dozen Magnolia Warblers
climb down white wind to the feeder that swings
from a skinny ash tree. They are a yellow I've never
seen before, black and white wing bars, a ring of dusky
gold above the small slope of the breast. Inside,
I consider curtains left by the woman who lived here
before me, delicate, snow-colored, perfectly hemmed.
A crisscross of blooming rosemary travels the cloth's
whiteness many washings faded.

Sometimes I pity her, all the care
she took with the neat, taut rod slip, the little gathered
apron at the top of the sill. Why didn't she roam outside,
listen to birds in the field, come north
on some rumor of winter ending?
When I was a girl, I made my hands
strong, heard the force of the first lilac crack
ice off the stem, held dirt as if I cupped
the face of a lover. Is there some unnumbered star
left to discover? Thrill

of a season's sudden turn; slant light in a blizzard
between drifts and falling sky, where a world opens.
How easy it is to miss, moments taken up
by a cracked sea-green bowl, pieces I hold, weight
of a woman's life whose name I don't know, who left it
with a smaller sister bowl here in the cupboard.

Outside, black seed I broadcast creates
a pattern I can't make out. The day has no seam, no
painstaking embroidery. It melts and cracks and freezes,
a galaxy shook all over, a brightness,
blue-white. I begin to shrink, cabin-small, all angles and bones.

I want a warbler's color on my shoulder.
I would stop, take note of the dull gleam,
the female's markings,
a meaning.

I Make A Place Here

I make a place here for my body,
for the dark shoulder and the hard hip
I use for breaking into the world. There is so much
love in my teeth, so much that cannot be done
softly or gently. From the bed
of my mother and father, where semen shines
on the woman's thigh, and the man curves
away from her, a slope in the dark,
I take myself. I remember them both in the sharpness of my
elbows, in the umbilical pull against my own gravity;
so many things call me violently to stand—
stones, white-notched bark of birches, dirt.
I sharpen the stick of my girlhood,
I make a place for myself,
my sex is filled with night, a rib
floats inside me, curved edge of a
young moon. I am located by breasts and bones,
by water. The ant crawls through sand building
my house. I live in the sand, with love and
self-cruelty, sticky with blood.
The thigh of my lover shifts, his pelvis
polishes my pelvis, I am weighed down.
I prepare myself each day to give birth,
out of lichen and the pine sap dried on the cone,
and the saw-throated crow, and speckled leaves
dying into the ground broken by my feet.
A daughter or son waits to be wrenched
through me from the rain.

Two

The Wild Field

There are too many faces as I move with the light
among breaths and heels and gestures,
from my life on one side of the street to
the opposite corner. Faces smudged by
the heart's exhaust, eyes heavy
with numbers, the small crowns of heads
of children. Faces stretched into angles
out of pain, skin turning the color of the city.
Tomorrow I won't be a woman, I'll be a horse.
Tonight I'll sleep without dreaming
of the cows I loved as a child.
There is no bridge to my mother, on her knees
in the beanflowers, she's drunk now.
There is no bridge to my father,
only a city.

An old man turns into paper on the curb
in front of me, old man with old teeth.
I touch the gray unrazored hair on his cheeks,
I hold on to his hands as they flatten
and vanish, I taste his life as I walk by him,
my tongue is tired, molars worn down by beef,
evictions, and jealousy; I can't spit it out,
there is no relief. The water-struck brick
of old buildings brings me to my knees,
the stopped clock in the blood, the codes,
the cards, machines that swallow me
flashing a sign on a screen in daylight, midnight
between avenues, bottles, shirts and books,
a net of hands and wishes, the intestines of
a drunk who crumples into nothing.

∽

A chair in a cafe is waiting for a man who will not come back,
its wooden legs have outlasted his arms,
there on the table is where he held a spoon,
there on the floor is space his feet took up,
the bones, the callouses, the arches.
At three o'clock the sun fills the window,
a man no longer squints at her wild yellow hair,
thousands of molecules redrift where his waist was.

∽

If there had been time I would have asked him...
Tomorrow I won't be a woman, I'll be a horse.

∽

How I love matter. How I love an eyelash, a tooth.
How I love feces, a bird at a window,
white-feathered and still at the glass.
I don't think it would trade
places with me, it is waiting
for me to vanish.
I press my forehead against the window
and the oil of my skin leaves a mark.
I would like that bird to lead me
through the city. I would like to comfort it.
White wings left their shadows on the tree
that stood where the window is.
I think sex is the only intelligence that lasts.

I keep thinking I see my brother at cross-streets,
wearing my father's hard shoulder, walking alone,
the sunlight carving his shadow on cement.
When I see him in the elbow or glance of a stranger
the mistake locates me by tears, I am definite
and weeping. I see the world in parts
since we aren't speaking; a leg, a wheel, a head-rag,
one word snapped like a wing from
the weight of its meaning.
Things are missing their relations.
Is there a law that remember his hands
when they were small and full of stars?
Who defines what I am? There is only
a sleeve broken off from its owner,
wind and a gutter of oil, a brother
no one sees.

Change, change, change, spare change, a woman repeats
from a vestibule, her voice lifts and dies.
I want to embrace her. The father and
mother in me say take care of each other.
Take care of the wet soles of old feet shining.
The world reflected in asphalt
blows back at the stars.

∾

I stand under an open window listening.
I run my hands along a fence slat and feel the teeth marks
of horses, at the edge of their field I whisper, let me in,
let me in.

∾

A star falls, an ovum lets go in my body,
lets go of the death in me, and the child.
Someone I love has died, his habits, his shyness.
Steam drifts from a street grate, white-mouthed and laughing.
I need to know what was done with his clothes,
the world of one yellow sweater has ended.
I was eating dinner when somewhere his heart stopped,
how good the bread tasted, and the water.
It takes so much light and time for one tomato,
a beautiful weight on the earth,
and dirt clings to onions in a field.
A man no longer speaks, his tongue no longer brushes
the silver in his teeth.

∾

Where is my sister?
I miss her in the follicles, the three depths
of my lungs, the lumbar.
What is the name of the city she lives in?
I miss my older sister, in the capillaries, the vagina.
What color has she dyed her hair?

There is a lilac branch in her shadow,
I carry its odor everywhere.
I miss my older sister, I am the witness to her puberty.
She was not kind, often women are not,
and young girls guard the sexual minerals they need.
It is so hard to lie down at the end of the day,
the ferocious atoms of a woman lie down,
the residue of soft acts and dreams,
yes to lie down

∽

A child is making pacts her life will hold her to,
with sand and metal, the red eyes of pigeons,
the father's voice and the voice of the mother,
actual or wind-grafted, alive in bone and in kisses
or built from a wheel and a leaf.
She jumps from the second step of the stoop
and falls, surprised by the weight of her body.
Didn't I fall through the veins of my father?
Didn't I race in a cell to be born?

∽

After midnight,
someone is singing in the snow,
the street is suddenly empty
except for that black haired boy
riding a bicycle home from his last delivery,
the knee-press, the song, the turning wheels.

⟳

A horse in my dream woke me.
I stood by its side in the dark.

⟳

Who are you walking toward me,
the sun in the material of your bones?
You have secrets no one else has told me.
I want to know if your father
lay his head down on folded arms
and cried in a kitchen alone.
What did your mother make out of her anger?
Was the first hint of you electricity clinging to her hair
as she brushed the day into place?
Was love already making a swing in her belly to hold you?

⟳

A rabbit hangs by its feet in the butcher's window.
A policeman daydreams, his lungs are full
of the cold morning air.
I have stolen his horse,
he does not know me.

⟳

Who are you?
More than this, more than this.

I need aluminum and time.
Someone I love has died.
Spring etches its leaves in the wind,
my fingernails grow,
my shoes press to the ground.
I have to conceive a child, now,
at this instant and no other,
loneliness has broken me down,
and time comes apart between
my thumb and my finger.

A horse is not naked or wild.
But a woman is,
and a man is.

I climbed out of the cradle of my own bones.
I felt the water break at my birth.
I made my compass from the hummingbird's
needle, from the stork's beak.
My father was sleeping,
my mother carried my death in her teeth.
A calcite flower is in my mouth,
I am sexual and ignorant
in a world of veins and metal.
Tell me what your cup and spoon does
when your back is turned.
What prayer should I say

over a dying stone?
Inherit me,
you do not know
how I love you.

⌇

A woman stands in clover and damp grass,
deeper than florescent city grass.
She has slipped off the bony back of the day,
she has lowered her tired shoulder
and walked without shoes into the pasture.
She doesn't want to be a woman.
She doesn't want to be a man.
The grain of a hoof is inside her, and powerful lungs,
and mare's breath.
Seven horses listen. They balance their shadows on the grass
under the naked stars.
I don't know if they are waiting for rain.
I don't know if they are waiting for fire.
What I don't know doesn't matter.

I felt the great ribs dissolving inside me.
Gone, the odor of summer from my hair,
skin on which the flies rode,
the black gleam of their bodies
in mustard weed, its seeds
blown every way in the wind
to bloom in the white skull
of who I was.
I remember.

Three

Wild Roses

The tide creeps in over gold
and rust-red sand, its low water warm at my ankles.
Crabs scale the floor's ridges in light.
The flat road to the bay is empty but for a few
swift shadows of clouds, hedges of beach plums,
the fruit heavy in the tight skin of summer, dense
around the seeds.

I follow the wild rose here. It grows without grandeur
on ridges of dunes, through weather-beaten fences.
I've always loved it, leafy stemmed, light flushed
in July heat. Wild in storms, the heart at home
in the rain. A flower full of breezes, the scent
not as sweet as other roses.

Younger, I studied it, the way a girl studies women,
for signs, secrets of the world around them.
For strength and heat, the hardness in the eyes that flickers
and is gone, sets the lips beneath the smile,
says I know what to expect this time,
when the wind is empty of the last trace of summer,
like the rented house of a lover.

I've hardly loved at all.
I've gathered petals from the dark road,
held bone-white pieces of shell to my mouth
to taste the whiteness.
I've taken a man in the middle of the day,
how my hips bruised him,
like the beach plum softened by the long days,
the color deepening on the stem
after the roses are gone.

This is the knowledge I've wanted.
The sticky marriage between finches
and the sweet decay of fruit.
I want the power of memory,
of acts never repeated
in just the same way,
the brief shadow on my shadow
across the asphalt road. Foam ringing the bay.
Wild roses.

Virgin

It is the odor I remember,
faintest scent of musk, as if an animal had entered
the room, a skunk following shadows at the end
of a long midwestern summer. Wet clover,
rags blackened by new oil for the high-priced
equipment of farms,
the first red leaf in the wind-break,
with its shadow like a hand
or a star.

I did it because my older sister
had done it. I didn't know what men were,
how they could bear the wrinkled pouches between
their legs. I couldn't stand to look at him,
panting and sweating under a mop
of rough, black hair.

It was like nothing at all.
No pleasure.
The memory of his swelling in my hand
as if he had been wounded there.
Salt.
I was alone with the private ceremony
of my body.

Winter came on. The dry smell of snow,
crop litter on the long, white fields.
Then spring, another summer.
All this entered me. Heat like a kind of gravity,
the marriage of corn,
the sound of the casing stripped back early
because I couldn't wait,
stood hidden there with the green threads,

crickets, the stain of the season on my legs,
as if I had been running through it forever.
I held the rough leaves of stalks in my hands,
whispering, reading
love letters.

Letter

I wrote that letter with both
of my breasts, I wrote it with my thighs
and my anus, with the whites
of my fingernails, the lines
on each side of my eyes.
I wrote it with a woman's sex,
red clitoris, and wiry pubic hair.
With hatred I reached over fear,
over water too deep, too swift,
the black broken jewel of my girlhood,
the odor of his decayed heart.
I made it on foot
with plump cells wild in my blood,
I picked up a pen instead of a knife,
and the naked places of my life shone,
the hollow between my legs, the hole
my urine flows through, the roots
of veins that flourish by the banks
of bones. I wrote it
with feces, the residue of all
that nourishes me. I wrote it with
acids that break down husks and stalks,
by the mineral light, the shadows
in back of the iris, the bird
of paradise that stirs in the white
nest of the brain.
I saw the sexual flower buried in ice
and said I will not destroy you.
I wrote a letter.
I sent him a fist, five knuckles
covered with the good salt
of mercy without forgiveness.

Blood

I look away until the tube of blood
is drawn, and then want to take the dark liquid back.
I see it is rich, I reach out for it like a lonely sister.
There is a light in my blood that is lost among the slides and racks.
How cold it is there,
how still without the noise of my body.
I touch the bruise on my vein,
the forgiving skin that closed so quickly.
My blood doesn't know I am only one person.
It warms me like summer on a stone.
It runs beside the bones of whoever I love,
it does not care who my father was,
I might have had many fathers.
It keeps my heart wet, turns black in the wind,
threads through the fat of my breasts, does not sleep.
I want to be better prepared for its beauty,
now that some of it has been taken from me.
I want to remember the sexual blood inside me long before
the days in the month when it falls.
I want to offer my embrace in its name,
because it came to me for no reason,
and is steady in my sadness.

These Eggs

I carry them up old stairways
into unfamiliar rooms, I lie down
with them on a blue and white bedspread,
and talk to myself openly about the future.
These eggs survive my hatred of my mother,
of the way she placed a hand
on her belly, as if it was the belly
of a stranger.
Hatred of the legs that opened,
the body that let me go
alone with my own body.
I wanted to be born from my father,
without blood, without trouble.
I carry these sticky flowers inside me
without feeling their weight.
I do not fall when they fall.
I do not know what their shadows look like.
One day I'll have a child,
a child who may hate me.
For my sake two people lay down
and touched bones.
And I'll lie down with light
on the long bones of my thighs.
I'll marry my shoulder to a man's shoulder.
I'll live my life around
the uncreated dark
of these eggs.

Soup

The mushrooms and barley weigh almost nothing
on the spoon. The liquid is salty. It tastes
like the wind at the corners of buildings,
like the water of my eyes, rain
for the skin of my face and the bone of my jaw.
But it's snowing outside now, not raining
and the soup warms me.
Once a boy held me on the porch steps
in summer and said *the world will hurt you*
because you don't see the world.
His worry was like the worry
of mothers for dreamers who carry
themselves out of the dream each day.
It's good to be awake and eating slowly by a window
looking out on the street. No one in this room
and no one outside walking knows my name,
knows that I am thirty,
am frightened and happy, that today
I am not ashamed of how long it takes me
to move through my life, having to look
at everything twice, three times, or more.
Eating is such a simple act, but it reminds me
of things I don't understand.
I don't understand
why I love the taste of the soup
that stays in my mouth
after I have put down my spoon
and dusk has been shrugged on by the day
and people walking hold the front of their coats
to their hearts.

Solitude

The night is already half-gone.
When I was a girl, and afraid, I would touch
my leg, or breast, touch skin and hair.
I thought my body held me as a house
holds a sleeping child.
The trucks rattle down Hudson Street.
My fingers smell of sweat,
and of sexual fluid, subtle and real,
entirely itself. I've wanted so much
for things to be like other things.
A young girl thinks her body
is a house, but the hands she held
in front of her face bled when
her mother beat her.
There was a man I thought of
as a bridge. I kissed his lips,
each hard rib. I wanted physicalness
to carry me over the water of my life.
But love frightened me.
Earlier, touching myself, I tried
to think of things as beautiful
as the body; coral,
inner pear, wild grape hanging
from the umbilicus of vine
in a cold season. I tried to remember
a whole day from childhood.
I've forgotten so much,
I'll forget this night, words I said,
the rushing shine and sudden
gravity—tea-rose, marsh foam,
salt, a man now asleep or awake
in another city, who came in me
saying *I'll miss you.*

Sleeping Together

Two women stand on the grass with their children
and I think of how last night I made love using nothing
to stop the semen from meeting the clear egg that clings
to my side. How I opened my mouth to his mouth as if we
were both trying to speak to the life we carry inside us,
in the blood shadow, the arterial lace, the mucous lights.
The driest cells of my skin sloughed off with his,
and the fluid of my sex turned silver in the darkened room
and he touched the edge of my uterus, the milk on the head
of his sex warm as breast milk. And I moved to receive it
as if the future did not exist, I pulled those bright fish in
as if I had no power to conceive, some part of me unborn in the heat,
something else that I needed. I lay there dumb as a fetus, loving
his scent, our weightlessness. And did not say how frightened I was
in the middle of the month when the minerals thicken,
when the ovum falls under the cold Pleiades,
gluey and speechless, until it is out of me, away from
my lost responsibilities. When I was a girl
my mother told me I was a mistake,
I did not know what it was like to be chosen.
Who might this man and I create together, out of his long thighs,
the ribboned vein on his bad knee. Out of my broad back,
the stitch in my side. There are so many lights
in the body's watery cells, who wouldn't want to live there
for a while. It's my life freed from the salt sack
that scares me, to ask for what I need, to learn how to speak.
Each night he and I sleep together we grow heavier,
the bed roots itself deeper into the multi-colored dirt
of pigeon feathers and sand, clay that shapes my dreams.
The sheets smell more of sky and our bodies speak, each
crevice and plane and hump, as we snore and breathe, and the stars
that drag the season forward flicker across the ceiling.

Out there in the dark another life starts
toward us, a fingernail flashes in the leaves,
an eye opens and weeps.

Wishes

I've wanted gentler arms,
twilight arms of a man and a woman
who cry when the sun lies down
on the river, and the boy sweeping
the sidewalk falls in love with the sound
of the broom, unaware that the moon has come out.
I've wanted a heart
in the naked float of my body
that would not wait too long
to come down,
down from fear, down
to the other, the genital home,
the man with his boyhood sleeping inside him,
and weightless hair under his arms,
and testicles so strange and real.
To be a woman, with a man, walking
though we are tired,
with seeds and gold urine,
into the dark.

Four

The Woodpile

We stack a cord of wood in the shed,
a gray shingled lean-to on its knees in dry grass.
An afternoon of carrying together
in wind that blows brightness back to the sun,
as if light rose first
from rusted leaves of burrs, prickly
blossoms on upward winding stems,
from mud in the dooryard shimmering.
Each log seems to weigh the same,
though they came from different trees,
some so green the heartwood bleeds,
some dry with field spiders
clinging to the sleeves of bark.
As we work, the spur in my heel hurts,
a temple of bones holds me up,
calcium arches rise. Behind us,
needles of tamaracks glow. I'm willing
to be happy, though it frightens me
these moments won't last; the man
who passes between shed and truckbed,
the space where we meet midway, our hips
that change places as the woodpile diminishes.
Not one of the logs we criss-cross
will be here in summer. Who would have thought
the coals could warm us so, the wood pop
as red comets trail up the flue.
Our bodies leak such sweet fluid, nerve endings
redden in the heat, as we move together
and more of the future disappears.
Day wears through to evening,
white brush stirs in a pool of shadows.
Light lets go of itself all over
the painted sky. Black lace of ants

skitters up a dome of sand, all the wood
is stacked. Last year's litter on the damp
shed floor shines; fox skull, gull feathers,
minerals being born.

Double-Stitched Quilt

On the wall above our bed, a quilt hangs, a pattern
stitched out of the past with a name I don't know,
maybe Tumbling Blocks, Drunkard's Path.
The woman who fell asleep
with the knowledge of the needle's progress
is gone. In the night-window white
and yellow blocks mirror and shine;
a thousand tiny measures of thread
telegraph her story.

Two days back at Shackford Head
I found a slender finger-bone
and brought it home. It tap tap
taps from the center of my hand, index
of a stranger's dreams. Water froze
at the spring mouth there, I walked to the lookout,
lichen in the seams of fire stone,
ghost of a volcano at the head
of the bay.

Sometimes I stop to feel the flannel at my wrists,
it's being touched by the world that I love,
cloth that circles my flesh and blood.
I sewed all I know on the quilt cover.
My husband asked, how can a crow turn to gold?
The loops between hem and border
flew off to the parson's roof,
cawed about what
a woman can do.

I am afraid to look in the button box
my mother gave me. Inside, a mouth opens, a child
will go hungry the rest of her life.

Here are whipping days, broken sticks of rages.
A girl with a home-made baby doll plants it
head first in the sand. Here are delicate stems
of old-lady glasses, split lenses to look
forward and backward. The past diminishes
the haunted land of her love.

Once this quilt was pieced
for warmth, beneath it a woman
dreamed. It was winter,
old brush whiskered straight up in snow,
grieving wind blew white roses on the window,
a quarter-moon outgrew its pointed skin.
She found it drying in the back field
and brought it in. The rest of her days
she lived stained by its shine.

The Fishwife

Loneliness has stolen my blouse and skirt,
there is nothing between my nakedness and sky, the curved sliver
of moonlight, a bright herring in black brine.
I'm a wife, a belly without a child, my hair done up in a net
of stars as I slit the cold seam at the fish farm, scales
sticking to me. My heart beats in the narrow
reeking body, among heaps of tin, crushed cans and bent lids,
labels that say nothing of my hobbled legs,
arrhythmic fins on the slick floor, eggs dark, obsidian.
Here I break the backs of blue mussels, am bleeder and cutter.
When the tide rolls away high water and foam,
another world appears. Freshets scrawl runes on the mudflats.
I walk out among periwinkles, green planets.
And forget the name of the town I come from, the cannery blast,
callous from the knife heel, home loves and disasters.
Dulse covers me, coiled sand worms become veins for my blood.
I'm other, instead of foreign. The smell of my own wetness
rises from slippery ground. Then the wheeled track of
pink starfish vanishes. The lid of the day comes down
against the pointed firs. I become a woman, ordinary,
in the wake of the water, my boots make a sucking noise
as I pull each foot from the sand.

Halley Farm

I follow the old demarcations,
a road with a name no one remembers,
walls of field stone fretted
with vine. The work of digging out
a cellar, laying beams
still claims this ground. Crows
sluice through cold wind where an orchard was.
I mimic a strange harvest of bringing in,
of the stem pull and bushel smell, the flat taste
of seeds buried in the core,
blossoms tight in the packed buds of winter.
Someone stood here, her hands
in gloves darkened by labors. She may have loved
the rough palms, the damp grasp of the interior.
As the harshness in her voice carried
did she cleave to the ache in her shoulders
at day's end, sister the edges of fields
with fever-few and beans? Look what it has come to—
weeds scramble the fence row, the door is gone,
hoarfrost winnows the hollow of her jaw.

I crave order.
Sometimes I shriek to the field light
and day moon—*just stop*
what you are doing, let me find a place for my fear.
The sleek, purple cases of milkweed shrivel,
my own face surprises me with its changes,
and I understand women who measure time
by men and children.
As I cross the crumbled threshold,
twilight blows down the frame the sun made
out of unfettered grasses, hogbed, bittersweet.
It may be she never dreamed

the cropped land would come back. I imagine her
taking a hand to one knee, tracing a finger on
the hard cap of bone, thinking
how odd I am, musing a legacy
for whoever wanders here.
True night throws a shadow across the hill,
my boots cut a rim in the dirt, my toes
touch the future.
And nothing I do
stops that.

Strawberries

This morning I ate strawberries, tore the green stem
from the soft body. I picked my own
in a field once, from a long
row of summer, a dusk away
from being over-ripe,
the sweetness darkening,
losing its shape.
I hated summer then, the clumsiness
of my knees in dirt.
I hated my heavy shadow,
moving sideways across
a line of green.
Leaves were the only coolness. They were like water,
the place in the pond colder
than all the other places, where night
was hidden or rain.

Men have always touched me.
An uncle, a grandfather.
As if there was no time to wait, as if my breasts
were dark and sweet, almost rotting,
almost coming apart in the hand.
I could smell myself on men—
my skin like sour ground after rain, white
as a piece of shell the gull leaves in the garden.

Now I have a husband, a man who won't steal
my odors from me, of labors and salt.
He never compares me to summer
when he touches me.
There is no rain, there is no sex with the scent
of a little white flower. Just a man, with
the strange shape of a heart over his sternum.

He knows
how heavy I am, sometimes in the dark
when I can't see his face.
My knees fit again into the hollows of a field.
My tongue is dry in the decay of summer,
the thickness of odors. Memory like a death
in another season
glistens and stains.

The River

Pepper-bush, marsh grass, white tuft of swans, I run
past the half-undone pink azalea, petals on River Road
heaped against the curb. Noon heats the scent of the river,
winter's rot of leaves, old rains, a high cut field.
I feel as if I have stolen my body, almost
thirty years of teeth and hair and tears.

Sweat stings my eyes, slides down my face like tears.
I love this, a joy at the start, middle, end of the run.
I've gotten away with my thighs, with calves, with skin, almost
intact from the sad stories of an old man, of a road
that goes nowhere, passes neither love nor field.
My father was, himself, a road, both feet stuck in a dark river.

Immovable, no mudfish dozed, or cat-tails swayed in his river.
His warnings stuck to me, his tears—
how private they were, a paradise, a secret field
in his heavy body, of dark stumps, matted lashes I run
from, tongue of sand, eyes of glass, silence, until the road
is just a road and I am almost

at the turn of the river, almost
half-way down the black vein by the river,
green grape leaves, hot buds unfurled, shadow the road.
I know I desired him, the clump of his sex, his unshed tears,
the east and west of his fists that went nowhere, run
their memories through my fists that pump, past field

and water, past slant roof and high roof, field
the sharp blades mowed down, new hay sliced almost
to the root. It is not desire I run
from, desire is the true river,

where the face cracks and reveals the true face, tears
are real there, the road

is real, it ends, the road
of my father's life that surprised him so, with no field
to overtake in the slickness of respiration, sweat like tears.
Only a man in the stillness, shadowless, almost
crazed by all that moved away from him, river,
wife, son, daughter, love, run.

How I love moving at the height of the day, almost
noon, five-starred leaves, witch's broom bright yellow, a river
follows, and my father without moving follows, and I run.

The Names of The Flowers

Reading this book I see names I imagined as a child,
starflower, gold thread, wool grass.
When the snow melts, I'll walk on the heath
where the world I invented meets the blossoming here
in bladderwort and jewel-weed, in the shape of the man
sleeping beside me, in the privacy of my own sleep
where the ear picks up what the heart is saying.
Friend, lover, fly-eating pitcher plant brought home
from the bog, saved from crumbling,
scattering.

Love takes my face off in front of the mirror: my body
dwarfed by the great green dresser, handpainted
before I was born. My mother watched her body change
at the same mirror. How steady was the hand
that drew the pink borders, around side drawers
open to private places in her life.
They smelled of salt-roses,
summer petals wind
scattered down the road.

She is old now. Milk stalk, devilwart. With the superstitions
of a daughter I throw salt over my shoulder when
she enters the room. Her hands tremble from the fault-
line of her life. She drags her mother's sex from the end
of a dried cord, wrinkled, turned inward,
like an ear. What did she listen to? What soft scarf
of desire lay knotted on her thighs. She brushed
the full bushes of hydrangeas and turned them blue,
in August, when the moon was hot and I lay
sleeping on my side, keeper of her secrets;
the mens' faces, the bleached fronts of old hotels.

In the bath my spine sinks to the white iron bottom.
Lilies on the wallpaper fade in a sky blue pond.
I am mad in love, gentle and barbed. This is not the water
I was born in, with its sulfur smell of egg and blackened
blood. Here the sex cradle is covered with foam,
green soap slips from the tin cup I keep
it in, metal mottled with stars. At love's threshold I put
an old iron stop by the door. My mother holds the skeleton key, she
weeps as I take my lover in at the root.

Time undoes me, my hair, my skin.
Lupine crumbles in the leaf-whipped fury of fall.
I pick my mother's curses off me. A woman of
bone, I recognize her death-house, her fingers
rattle as they motion me home.
I want to take her hands in mine,
the little love-me-knots of her cuticles, the white ridge
of her nails where she touched the moon to
show me it was real.

Two in The Morning

My kitchen shift ending,
I would feed the iron mouth of the dumpster
remains of strangers' dinners, leaves from heads
of a hundred lettuce, nets from frozen sides of beef,
the blood wan and cold, gristle and garnish, lipsticked
tissue, a napkin a drunk tried to write a letter on.
It was my favorite time of night, outside, away
from the heat of the grill, steam from the washer.
Frigid air turned my breath white, winter entered my body,
glassy faces of meters shone, and stars over the parking lot
blossomed against the dark curve of the earth. I wasn't
thinking of flowers, I was thinking my hands were as hard
as a man's hands, they smelled like the wooden block
I scored with my knife, like sticky skins of onions,
potato dust, the black dirt that clings to hearts and roots.
I was all muscle and dream. The distance between stars
was the distance between lives one person could lead
from birth to dying. In the privacy of sweeping and lifting,
in the cellar work where I uncradled greens someone's
back broke packing, I believed it was true;
my hands would not always carry the odor of work home,
my power was not a feast to be eaten, bit by bit.
So much light fell from the sharp shape of the moon, and I was
equal to its beauty.

Season

for Laurie

Beyond the rose-of-sharon tree,
where strange pale flowers reach
for me, I walk in the shade of maples
amazed by the cool green
light of leaves.
As a girl I took a path
soft as this path, unpaved, a line
in a grassy trench, never straight
or marked by some final destination.
Grandfather is dead. Grandmother has turned
to bone. Twenty years ago I walked
in the shadows between houses alone,
and I am still alone, even knowing
my husband stands by the old screen,
by garden gloss of marigolds,
tomatoes dropping heavily
on summer ground, going to sleep now.
I walk in softness, hungry
for the rot of fall, red apples
cold in their beds, the ancient approach
of winter. A child
swims up at me, thrashes
a strange tide, impatient for me
to wake to its birth.
I conceive it here, first,
in the trunnels of early evening,
to the rhythm of insects rubbing, a sound
humans set their pulses by.
So the child will survive all I have
lost, the odor of wild onion
my hands held, unkindness,

and feral blood, to walk unknowing
through the thick descent of dusk,
and love the earth.

Laundry and Wind

Wind blew through the open door of the laundromat,
wind that puts seeds on the tongue of a woman, wind for the water
of the body, breast-wind, hip-wind, heel-wind. How delicious
it is to grow older in a wind like this, though my father will die, and
my mother is younger than I am, maternal to flowers.
I filled my mouth with dirt from her garden when I was a girl,
hoping she would bend down to me. Wind brushes my knees,
cool through the clothes I wear in the naked world,
wind tickles my jaw.
Regret is a curved shape, an ovum with no name
that shines as it falls. I stoop to pick up
the socks dropped on the floor, my spine curves among
the edges of old washing machines.
Wind for my teeth, wind for my underwear,
wind for the soap that cleans the smell of God
from the armpits of shirts.
I can't eat the wind, or make love to the wind.
I cover it with kisses and the kisses
blow back to me. I am grateful for self-love,
at the laundromat, or in the dark, or on the street.
The smell of bleach makes me think of a clothesline,
tied between the posts of my early life,
a shadow of a line I walked on with my eyes closed,
asking, who am I?
Who is the Uncle lighting matches at my nipples like a blind man?
What becomes of the child who grows up among thieves?
Wind for the poor, wind for the sick, wind for the rich.
All my life I thought I was ugly.
A dryer spins warmth into my sheets,
white cloth stained by my menstrual blood,
my flag. Do I look like a kind woman?
I dreamed I killed my elders,
it was a dream of health.

I fold my favorite skirt slowly as the wind
works a spell on me.
Wind for this room full of strangers.
Wind for the man whose pockets are full of quarters.
Wind for the pregnant woman holding a warm
pillowcase to her cheek.
Wind for me at thirty washing.

I am grateful to the following people for their encouragement and help during the preparation of this book: Stanley Burnshaw, Nancy d'Estang, Shawn Johnson, Laurie Kutchins, Timothy Liu, Margaret Lloyd, Charles Martin, Donna Masini, Regina McBride, Catherine McDonald, and Madeline Silber.

Alice James Books has been publishing poetry since 1973. One of the few presses in the country that is run collectively, the cooperative selects manuscripts for publication, and the new authors become working members of the press. The poets are the publishers, participating in every aspect of book production, from design and editing to paste-up, from consultation with printers to distribution and marketing. The press was named for Alice James, sister of William and Henry, whose gift for writing was ignored and whose fine journal did not appear in print until after her death.

Recent Titles:

Margaret Lloyd, *This Particular Earthly Scene*
Jeffrey Greene, *To the Left of the Worshiper*
Alice Jones, *The Knot*
Nancy Lagomarsino, *The Secretary Parables*
Timothy Liu, *Vox Angelica*
Suzanne Matson, *Sea Level*
Cheryl Savageau, *Home Country*
Jean Valentine, *The River at Wolf*